AF413118

My Bond

My Bond

Joshua L Jorgensen

CONTENTS

A
Nameless Love

HeartShade

She is a visceral force stirring my heart to surrender flutters of affection. Her beauty welled effervescently, pushing for perfection possible. Her imaged affect tunnels sight losing my sense surmise of time. Moments slip reality, bending memory integrity leaves me elusive to lucidity.

Earned her traits from the Fae, distorting perceptions by mere glance upon her semblance. Spelling divine sexuality by subjugating visual ecstasy. She radiated a proverbial seductive heist, thieving all resistance submits my existence.

Her body bejeweled garnet figured deep set in desire. She pulls me closer with delicate cambers leading me to candescent contours, stammering my composure she relentlessly solicits for. I found myself smitten in complacency with senses dancing implicit verve. To behold a sight set on her begets a homage to her heavenly visage.

Blessed incitements flowed over my mind, inspiring I could meet with her. I contemplated an impromptu for resolve my endearments I confess with subtle flattery. I'll ask my heart to profess unite in near sight future date. Now speak, my hope inherit.

The Widow

My anatomy draws in close a catch. Chance for vibrations breaking stillness slept. Strands strum bass in tone a desperation shown. Revealing opportune off eight my eyes. I delight to bite the squirming fright. Quick I prick my meal just right. Silken coffin confection filled with blood. Visions of vitals undulates to circulate alive in me. Mind the author of my urge, confidence enacts a court to congress with her.

My bride displays a disarming unstirred guise. An entrapment of besetting beauty beheld my instincts affair, she's perfect art composed by nature. I wildly dreamt of her while invoking indifference towards danger, signs I ciphered as unclear. Mindful what harms could carry but only for fears to fall short of assumptions, if pain could lack affliction. And what is a future if not known, a predicted notion for choice and taste. Relief in fantasy built my imaginate can be known as real. She moves with an entrancing embodiment of allure beckoning me closer. She whispers in hiss, "My catch is not for want but is willed to be mine. The child of nature "Death" was named from all life birthed became."

There I see she holds my hand, this vision enchants a perceived foretelling. I then pluck for your traps, my allowance for advance. What awaits my future is just ingress. Life with no purpose could not be life nor purpose without life, find this you won't see. My purpose found, short lived but infinite then indefinite ease to oblivion. No longer moved to calculate, becomes me a taste for you. Death a lie, it was life you whispered to me my Widow.

The Fears
in
Reflection

Phantom

The body endures for the mind contests against manifests. The looming pendulum of time slices and bleeds splintering flesh. Following bane or fame grabs for a past once had. Reemerged wounds impulse to confide in lies. Silent in the light-less, grins stays well hidden. Has a face shameful shown in light. Terror built born from fright. Closer who I'll feast upon who less sense me presently. An unrelenting pursuit hides behind eyes my unnatural fess, I brood deceit if met. Thirsts for comfort, could be a Love but foreign perceived by glares declares "Envy". Sewn in vengeance, leads down roads of ruination so saith I, "Must be mine and not for another."

I dwell between spoken and the seen. The trusts of the many will lead down road's ensnares. Liar am I will surely listen, and my disguise for one will follow. Poisons are the versing phantom, inducing forms of panic. Rips into wants and finds what I seek. The nature of life I eat upon, holding death in one hand and teeth. "Envy" is a predator admitting my place in nature. Takes without a wish, wishing needs are hoping.

Blinded I'm self possessed, peering thru selfish spirit bindings.
Knows a fall to come if by own will desired. Has a mind not
far from the free, speaks from fears and rallies to convict.
"Envy" learnt from Death, no need to claim a side.

Awaits for breath, a sigh is relief. Stays alone so one only
knows.

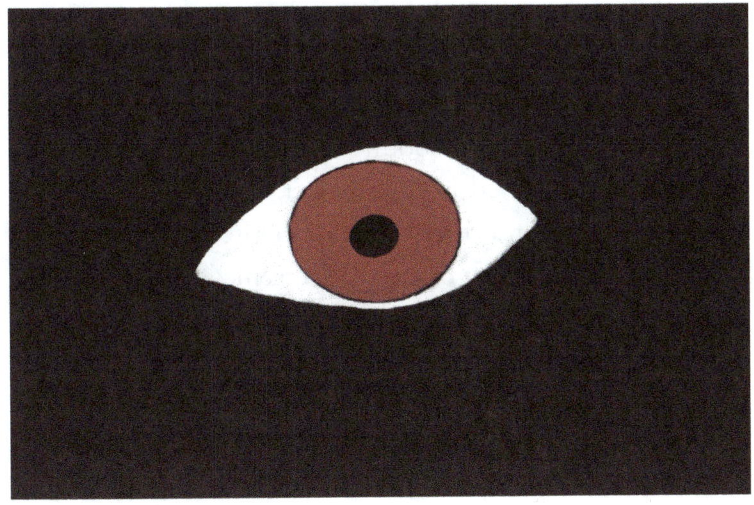

Pop

Listening in silence paints pursuits for sources unspoken. My curiosity filled by dread and apprehension foretold tales of a feminine aberration, thus is my current present muse. A foreboding presence emanated in me, forming my anxious accord. Then with affected fear, faint sounds of weeping could be heard, with disdain to escape her prison of solitude. I faced her unnerving and wide eyed. Wherefore she carried herself, a dissonance followed. She is traced in a seeming smoky visualization. She knowingly possessed a curse of spirited reanimation, I begrudged and felt retribute for her. She appeared still and bound by an existence revealing her relapse of a once lived life alas is lost. Her display of countenance clear beyond reverie. With inherited afflictions from death, how the warmth of a touch is seemed foreign and forever but to never forgotten the feeling. Repression remained in her absolute. To live as a void and absent of entropy, her will is lost in past strife. Death holds her in a grip of darkness, rejecting the light of a new day. Accepting fate in the ephemeral. She reverbs the walls pleading, "To be bled once more, to be alive never more."

She molds herself from ethereal, by collecting memories the repeats of her past. What remains in memory are moments to appear beyond the veil. She pulls away from hope convey, forbidding freedom by dismay. Bound to the mise of death's mast she'll forever portray.

Path
of
Hope

Memories

Wheresoever I go, immersive memories last. Refuse myself a devouring past, never-ending hunger of times alas. And alas my collective is a lens perspective. A focus curved in stirred with malice. Plea I flee my mind's ingress, this mask is worn now frowns too fast. I ask what should I seem appear, my memories are fraught with rue dismay. I wither and shrivel in shadow my pain. Unbearable fates, are the plights my sickness makes. Deep are my roots, I'm lost in darkness. Which way is life? I fight for each breathe raught shallow and tight.

I pray for hope having colors compliment each other, inspire conversing from within the heart. A stillness quiet preludes a song of insight singing symphonies, "You shall not faulter focus for bright is my Light. Persevere and blossom beyond traced fright. Mustering growth, never sever upright. Whereby each petal unfolds a framework inlay bloomed perfect in sound and sight. Your best has yet will soon take flight."

Hope now reveals me wholly resolute and memories no longer abide me sold.

Pebble

Prayer perfects my joys. Then better I'll be when meaning gives perceived, I'll sought to spare a care. As do wisdom walks above the world of wants, displacing weight for thanks and font.

Could hope be the size of a pebble, dense in possibility ergo indefinite value. Forgo of any trade cause loss will give a cost. This pebble calling for caliber, all is bold whom hold. Having one, two could follow lest a fraught and loss by phantom. When one speaks truth heard by one, then two could not have fathomed. Beyond my eyes and touch proclaims, perfect is one profound in hitori.

Truth is beauty worthy for one. Aware the frail naïve as youth has shown, destructive qualms blinds eyes who trust on loan. Amid the dire of fire obscene, be close my pebble our faith holds us together.

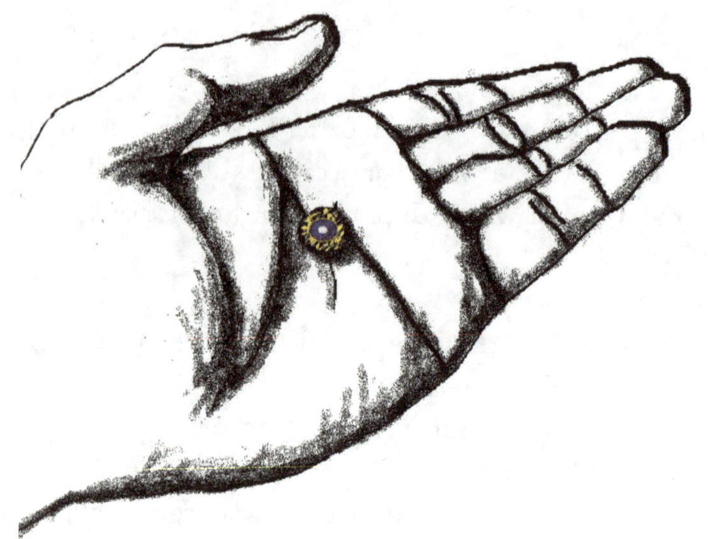

Sewn This Thread

Time

Time descants rhythmic symphony ensembles. Confined to cause impending flaws but hope convicts made flesh symbolic. We're born with a gem, safe inside but the world forsakes. Each gem rests within till each their end or one undo. Rebuke who scoffs their names are Faust. Each step will stride towards fate. Pulled by strings impending scenes if choice all dies and never dream.

Tidings are for follow and silence adheres, objective the mind finds times fallible binds. What bends between unknown foreseen, so sow your night by day will change. A Love certain unseen from bane, outside of time two hearts combine. Pride is bound to shame confound. Kindness shapes in selfless hands, reveals a Hope sealed from sight. Whence moments come less and lesser nigh comes say, "Protect your gem and words of Hope, you'll never fall short hence forth good wealth."

Binary

The will made spoken ponders spells yet seen. Spells are from the spirit speaking letters, feeding readers soothing caters or raping seether. Layer a thick intent lest be the one possessed and plagued in mind. Suffering scenes embodies fiends, inching closer towards the ends each hold. Cause the mind's insight borderlines the surface outside. Receives receipts the soul has seized folding in on everyone else but mine. The world weighs truth as binary, never counting two.

Reluctant to share my dreams has caused me held and bound, "Unlikely" once said. Then give me lists of disposition, my character with a name. Tell me who I am before I do, if fate was spite. Then piece your temp to me as if Truth is meant to be spent, my adherence will not pledge devotion. Say your sight to see for me, you forget hope draws from honesty. Before farewell I'll ask to trade for Truth, I hope you'll say "No."

You see the compounds of my chemicals, the demise to deterior. Should the upmost stability be faith, then prescription's no fine.

Prescription Receipt

01100110 01100001 01101001 01110100 01101000

Cost: $0.00

www.ingramcontent.com/pod-product-compliance
Lightning Source LLC
Chambersburg PA
CBHW050746150726
48196CB00004B/359